$1.50

Treasury of *Satsuma*

Price Guide

Sandra Andacht

DATE DUE

738.37
And

0048088
COPY 1

Cumberland Trail Library System
Flora, Illinois 62839

738.37
And

Prices vary in different regions of the United States, as well as in various countries throughout the world. The main factors governing prices at the present time are supply, demand, and the profit margins dealers have set for themselves. It would be beneficial to use the following criteria, in the order given, when setting values or making evaluations as to merit and value. This criteria was used in correlation with prices gathered from various regions of the United States and countries throughout the world for formulating the value ranges given in this guide.

- Age
- Availability
- Size and Contour
- Style and Method of Decoration
- Quality and Workmanship

The purchaser must weigh two factors before making a final evaluation as to the worthiness of a particular piece. First, the initial time and effort afforded to the creation of said object must be considered. Second, using the criteria above as a guide, the relationship of a particular object to its price tag may be further refined. A combination of these two factors should lead to a reasonable assessment of the value of a given example of Satsuma.

1. (L to R) Water droppers —
   $350-500; $350-450;
   $375-500
2. Water dropper — $950-1,200
3. Dish — $400-650
4. Ewer — $1,000-1,300
5. Bottle — $1,800-2,300
6. Vase — $1,500-1,700
7. Bottle — $900-$1,200
8. (L to R) Cha wan — $500-600;
   $550-650; $500-600
9. Saucedishes — $200-300, each
10. Tile — $400-500
11. Tea set — $850-$1,000
12. Vase — $900-$1,100
13. Kogo — $900-1,200
14. Bowl — $1,900-2,300
15. Teapot — $325-$425
16. Koro — $4,000-$5,000
17. Bottles — $1,200-1,500, each
18. Koro — $4,000-5,000
19. Vase — $2,000-2,500
20. Mizusashi — $10,000-13,500
21. Koro — $2,500-2,850
22. Koro — $2,000-2,350
23. Vase-koro — $600-850
24. Koro — $400-600
25. Cha wan — $450-550
26. Vase — $250-375
27. Vase — $250-325
28. Figure — $25,000+
29. (L to R) Figures — $3,500-4,500,
    each
30. Figure — $3,500-4,500
31. Tray — $900-1,200
32. Vases — $1,400-$1,600
33. Vases — $1,600-1,800
34. Bowl, covered — $1,500-1,600
35. Plate — $1,900-2,450
36. Figure — $6,000-8,000
37. Vase — $3,500-4,775
38. Jar — $4,000-5,000
39. Vase — $400-600
40. Teapot — $275-345
41. Pilgrim flasks — $2,700-3,200
42. Vase — $1,600-1,800
43. Bowl — $650-900
44. Bowl — $650-900
45. Vase — $1,800-2,200
46. Figure — $3,500-4,300

47. Tray — $2,500-2,950
48. Figure — $1,800-2,200
49. Figure — $1,700-2,100
50. Figure — $1,650-1,775
51. Figure — $1,800-2,200
52. Figure — $1,950-2,350
53. Figure — $4,000-5,000
54. Figure — $1,900-2,250
55. Figure — $1,100-$1,500
56. Vase — $700-950
57. Charger — $2,500-3,500
58. Bowl — $3,000-3,300
59. Plate — $3,402-3,700
60. Jar, covered — $3,500-4,100
61. Vase — $1,100-1,300
62. Vase — $1,600-1,950
63. Vases — $2,600-3,000
64. Bowl — $2,400-2,700
65. Jar — $10,000-12,000
66. Vase — $900-1,100
67. (L to R) Coffeepot — $500-700; teapot — $250-300; coffeepot — $450-555
68. Vases — $2,200-2,650
69. Koro — $1,200-1,500
70. Jar — $1,900-2,250
71. (L to R) Vases — $350-400; $300-385
72. (L to R) Boxes — $300-400; $250-325
73. Cha wan — $250-375
74. Vase — $1,500-1,700
75. Kogo — $350-500
76. Kogo — $650-850
77. Vase — $1,100-1,450
78. Vase — $2,300-2,850
79. (L to R) Top row: Vases — $2,000-2,500; vase — $900-1,100; vases — $1,800-2,100; vase — $1,400-1,600. Bottom row: Vases — $800-900; Koro — $3,000-3,500; vase — $600-800; Koro — $3,200-3,700; vase — $400-575

80. (L to R) Top row: Jars — $1,900-2,100; vase — $800-1,000; vase — $1,900-2,300; vases — $3,100-3,450. Bottom row: Figure — $1,900-2,400; figure — $1,900-2,400; vases — $1,400-1,600; bottles — $2,800-3,150; figure — $3,000-4,000
81. Koro — $3,000-4,000; charger — $3,000-3,500
82. (L to R) Vases — $3,000-4,000; charger — $3,000-3,500
83. Vase $1,200-$1,500
84. (L to R) Vase — $400-500; teapot — $250-300
85. (L to R) Top row: Tea set — $150-175. Bottom row: Box — $300-400; teapot — $300-350; pitcher — $100-125
86. Brush pot — $175-220
87. Vases — $2,200-2,500
88. Jar — $700-900
89. (L to R) Bottle — $125-155; bottle — $155-175
90. Jar — $350-450
91. Bottle-vase — $600-800
92. Tea caddy — $350-500
93. Jardiniere base — $950-1,200
94. Vases — $1,800-2,200
95. Cricket cage — $600-775
96. Vase — $125-145
97. Ewers — $1,450-1,600
98. Vase — $700-875
99. Saki pitcher — $675-900
100. Vase — $600-800
101. Jar, covered — $600-800
102. Figure — $5,000-6,000
103. Bowl — $250-285
104. Bowl — $200-225
105. Bowl — $600-800
106. Shell — $145-185
107. Vase — $400-650
108. Bowl — $700-1,100
109. Saki pitcher — $700-875

Cumberland Trail Library System
Flora, Illinois 62839

110. Vase — $500-700
111. Vase — $200-300
112. Bottle-vase — $1,200-1,600
113. Bowl — $2,200-2,800
114. Bottle-vase — $500-700
115. Vase — $500-700
116. Koro — $800-1,100
117. Tea set — $350-450
118. Vases — $850-950
119. (L to R) Koro — $600-800; teapot — $200-250
120. Pitcher — $150-175
121. Bottle — $195-220
122. (L to R) Vase — $120-135; vase — $65-95; pitcher — $120-150
123. (L to R) Sugar bowl — $100-150; teapot — $95-120; cha wan — $70-90
124. Miniature jar — $200-300
125. Basket — $75-125
126. Jar-urn — $600-800
127. Vase — $600-800
128. Jar — $125-145
129. (L to R) Top row: vases — $600-800; vase — $350-450. Second row: koro — $350-450; jar — $800-900; vase — $400-425. Third row: teapot — $200-250; brush pot — $200-225; teapot — $320-350. Fourth row: vase — $300-400; vase — $700-950; pitcher — $175-210
130. Toothpick — $145-180
131. Vase — $60-90
132. Vase and pedestal — $1,900-2,400
133. Picture frame — $195-220
134. Bucket — $110-145
135. Saki cups — $120-140, each
136. (L to R) Salt — $45-50; pin tray — $25-35; saki pot — $95-125
137. Bowl — $500-600
138. Bowl — $800-1,100
139. Cha wan — $600-800
140. Master salts — $225-325, each
141. Koro — $450-500
142. Koro — $600-800
143. Koro — $1,200-1,400
144. Koro — $600-800
145. Koro — $900-1,100
146. Koro — $400-500
147. Kogo — $800-1,200
148. Koro — $125-150
149. Wine pot — $800-1,200
150. Cricket cage — $600-800
151. Tea set — $110-145
152. (L to R) Coffeepot — $125-175; teapot — $125-150
153. Vase-bottle — $350-475
154. Vase — $350-400
155. Vase — $200-350
156. Bowl — $125-145
157. Bowl — $300-425
158. Bowl — $225-300
159. Bowl — $110-135
160. Vase — $100-120
161. Vase — $250-260
162. Vase — $200-300
163. Vases — $200-300
164. Vases — $100-120
165. Vases — $110-135
166. Vases — $145-175
167. Vases — $200-250
168. Vase — $300-400
169. Toothpick — $400-500
170. Toothpick — $475-600
171. Vases — $600-800
172. Saki pitcher — $300-400
173. Vase — $400-485
174. Vase — $600-800
175. Saki pitcher — $400-500
176. Saki pot — $200-255
177. (L to R) Teapot — $600-800; teapot — $200-300
178. Partial tea set — $200-225
179. Vase — $160-220
180. Vase — $150-185
181. Vase-bottle — $175-200

Copyright 1978
Sandra Andacht

ISBN 0-87069-227-5
Library of Congress #77-80744

Published By

Wallace-Homestead Book Co.
1912 Grand Avenue
Des Moines, Iowa 50305

SATSUMA

An Illustrated Guide

By Sandra Andacht

234. (L to R) Top row: Tea set — $225-250. Second row: tea set — $325-375. Third row: Tea set — $275-300
235. (L to R) Top row: Tea set — $185-200. Second row: Saki bottle — $20-25; Demitasse set — $125-150. Third row: Juice set — $165-200. Fourth row: Vase — $40-45; cookie jar — $85-110; planter — $35-45
236. Small serving dish — $1,300-$1,500
237. Brazier (hibachi) — $1,800-2,200
238. Double gourd bottle — $1,100-1,350
239. Large bottle — $650-800
240. Tea caddy — $1,000-1,200
241. Koro — $550-650
242. Vase — $2,800-3,200
243. Teapot — $250-375
244. Mantle set — $1,900-2,100
245. Teapot — $275-380
246. Vase — $250-325

182. Vase — $300-4000
183. Vase — $120-145
184. Vase — $120-140
185. Vase — $145-160
186. Vase — $100-125
187. Vase — $100-125
188. (L to R) Vase — $85-100; vase — $100-110
189. Cup and saucer — $35-45
190. (L to R) Top row: Button — $75-90; button — $10-12. Bottom row: Button — $35-45; button — $135-150; pin — $160-200
191. Vases — $300-400
192. Vase — $1,300-1,500
193. Buttons — $1,000-1,100
194. Belt buckle — $200-225
195. Cigarette box — $65-90
196. Powder box — $50-75
197. Powder box — $400-500
198. Powder box — $600-950
199. Kogo — $1,100-1,500
200. Plate — $1,100-1,600
201. Kogo — $900, 1,200
202. Kogo — $900-1,200
203. Kogo — $900-1,200
204. Kogo — $400-500
205. Kogo — $600-800
206. Plate — $800,1,100
207. Box — $75-100
208. (L to R) Top row: Vase — $20-30; figure — $150-220; vase — $125-150; vase — $150-185. Second row: Vases — $300-400; bowl — 100-140; vase — $60-80. Third row: Vase — $25-35; vase — $80-90; vase — $95-110; vase — $100-125
209. (L to R) Top row: Vase — $75-95; vase — $150-175; vase — $60-85. Bottom row: Vase — $150-185; vase — $300-385; vase — $90-120
210. (L to R) Top row: Vases — $250-300; vases — $100-120. Bottom row: Vases — $250-300; vases (center) — $300-360
211. (L to R) Top row: Vase — $50-90; vases — $300-400. Bottom row: Vases — $400-500; vase — $125-140
212. (L to R) Top row: Vase — $150-185; vase — $100-140; vase $160-190. Bottom row: Vase — $135-150; vase — $175-210; vase — $150-175
213. Dish — $400-500
214. Bowl — $400-500
215. Dish — $340-400
216. Kogo — $600-750
217. Kogo — $1,000-1,400
218. Bowl — $500-550
219. Box — $400-465
220. Saki pot — $450-500
221. Jar — $900-$1,000
222. Nut set — $500-625
223. Sugar and creamer — $500-675
224. Vase — $200-300
225. Koro — $300-400
226. Bowl — $700-800
227. Bowl — $200-300
228. Bowl — $400-485
229. Kogo — $400-500
230. Koro — $300-400
231. Koro — $400-500
232. (L to R) Top row: Cup and saucer — $50-65; demitasse cup and saucer — $20-35. Bottom row: Dish — $20-30; syrup pitcher — $50-85
233. (L to R) Top row: Koro — $50-60; vase — $25-35. Second row: Teapot — $25-35; teapot — $25-35. Third row: Lamp base — $12-15; teapot — $25-35; lamp base — $12-15

CONTENTS

Foreword 5
Introduction 6
Dating 7
Symmetry 8
An Introduction to Marks 9
Marks and Symbols
    Marks Commonly Found on Satsuma-Style
        Wares 10-11
    Marks and (Mon) Crests Found on Satsuma
        Wares 12-14
    Symbols Found on Satsuma and Satsuma-Style
        Wares 15
    Additional Symbols 16
Helpful Hints 17
Color Photographs 18
Glossary 66-67
Bibliography 68

Dedication
To my dear friend, Irene Stitt.

Acknowledgements
My sincere appreciation to Mr. and Mrs. Charles Fendt, Mr. and Mrs. Ed Lewand, Mr. and Mrs. Stu Pearson, Mr. and Mrs. Milt Rabuse and Mrs. Irene Stitt, for allowing portions of their collections to be photographed.

Photography
Photographs by Daniel Stone.

Marks and Symbols
Marks and symbols were hand drawn by Carl Andacht.

Foreword

Satsuma and Satsuma-style wares are a unique art form within the realm of antiques and collectibles. Satsuma was painstakingly crafted by hand and so no two pieces are exactly alike. Satsuma-style wares were decorated by hand and therefore have only very basic similarities. Each and every piece of Satsuma and Satsuma-style wares was embellished with its own special character, charm and aura of beauty.

Introduction

Satsuma is a Japanese faience (glazed pottery), which is finely crackled and has a cream, yellow-cream or gray-cream color and is decorated with raised enamels.

Satsuma-style ware is Japanese porcelain which is decorated with raised enamels.

About 1600, after failing to conquer Korea, feudal lord Shimazu Yoshihiro returned to Japan, and brought with him approximately twenty-two Korean potters. These potters settled in Kushikino and Kagoshima, Satsuma Province, on the Island of Kyushu. It was these Korean potters that succeeded in making the first Satsuma faience wares.

Most of the Satsuma and Satsuma-style wares found today are produced in such places as Kobe, Kyoto, Tokyo, Kutani in Kaga Province and Awaji Island. (It is proper to call the same wares, made at different places, by the same name.)

Until the mid 1700s, Satsuma was an undecorated ware. When enameling was first used it was not ornate. Gold enamels were first added during the latter part of the 1700s, and were used sparingly. Most of the early decorations were floral designs with birds and butterflies. By 1800, geometric and other repetitive patterns (known as diapers) and landscapes were added to the overall designs.

It was approximately 1850 that human figures, warriors and saintly figures were first used as decorations on Satsuma wares. This figural Satsuma was made specifically for export. From the time of the Meiji Restoration (1868), they were sent abroad in large quantities. Their decorations conformed with the Western concept of Orientalia. Many of the motifs used on these wares and the later Satsuma-style wares are artistic interpretations of Japanese legends and myths and Buddhism. Figural Satsuma is not as scarce as the wares produced earlier, and they run the gamut from excellent to poor quality. Rejected by some past published authorities in the field of Oriental ceramics, figural Satsuma is no longer unacceptable. It deserves the same considerations and judgments that were given to earlier Satsuma.

Dating

The proper way to date Satsuma and Satsuma-style wares is to correlate each piece to the system used by the Japanese.

Edo period   1615-1868

The later years of the feudal age. The reign of the Tokugawa Shogunate.

Meiji period   1868-1912

The reign of Emperor Mutsuhito Meiji. The beginning of open trade with Western countries.

Taisho period   1912-1926

The reign of Emperor Yoshihito. A time of increased mass production.

Showa period   1926-present

There are two acceptable forms for dating. If the time period of a particular piece is known, it can be dated as follows: e.g., "vase, early Meiji period," or "vase, late Edo period." If an approximate date within a particular time period can be established, it is also proper to date as follows: e.g., "vase, Meiji period, circa 1890," or "vase, Edo period, circa 1820."

Symmetry

Satsuma wares were crafted by hand. One artist may have developed a piece or pair solely, or several artists may have worked on a pair or individual piece. An article may have been shaped on a potter's wheel or the clay may have been rolled into long ropes and then smoothed to form the proper shape. Enamels and designs were applied, for the most part, without stencils. This kind of craftsmanship causes irregularities in size, shape, glazing, enameling and design. However, these irregularities are not imperfections. In fact, they add to the value and beauty of Satsuma.

An Introduction to Marks

Marks were incorporated into designs, placed under bases, on rims of lids, on covers, bases and even on the interior of covers and lids. There is always a curiosity as to the meanings of the marks that appear on Satsuma and Satsuma-style wares. Those that are most readily found have been included. However, with the exceptions of Nippon, Made In Japan and Occupied Japan, marks are relatively ineffectual. For the most part, they can not be used to determine age or authenticity.

Marks and seals, written and incised, were bought, sold and openly copied. It was not uncommon for many generations of one family to use the same mark. Even the (mon) crest of the House of Satsuma appears on wares made elsewhere.

If a piece is unmarked or has Japanese characters, it does not mean that it is old. From 1891 to 1921, in accordance with the McKinley Tariff Act, the Japanese marked wares which were exported to the United States, "Nippon." Nippon (Japan), was used to designate the country of origin. During these years, paper labels were also used. They too were marked Nippon, but they were easily removed or deteriorated with time.

In 1921, the United States found the designation Nippon to be unacceptable. By the second half of 1921 the change was made and wares were marked Made In Japan." "Occupied Japan" was used from approximately September, 1945, after the signing of the Potsdam Declaration, until April, 1952, when the peace treaty went into effect.

Marks Commonly Found on Satsuma-style Wares

Used first half
of 1921

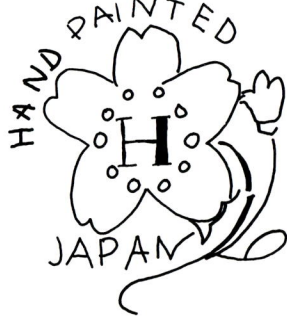

Plum Blossom

M in Wreath

Gold Castle

O.G. Japan

Pawlonia Blossom

Double T Diamond, Japan

Royal Satsuma Nippon

Marks and (Mon) Crests found on Satsuma Wares

1. Sixteen-petaled chrysanthemum. Used by the Imperial House.

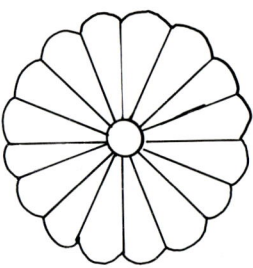

2. Dai Nippon ("Great Japan").

3. Kutani ("Nine valleys") Found on Satsuma-style wares as well.

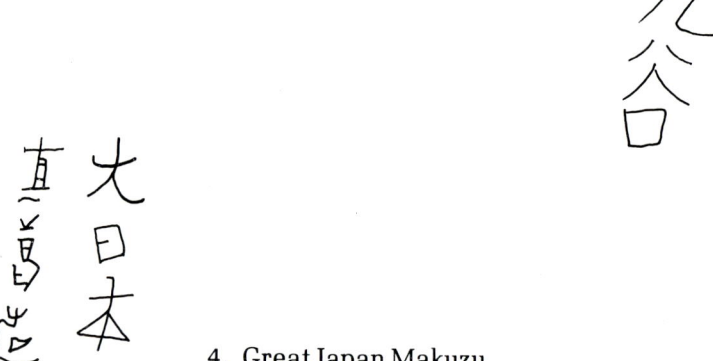

4. Great Japan Makuzu

5. Pawlonia Blossom, (Mon) Crest of the Empress.

6. Tanzan

Tanzan

7. Awata

8. Kinkozan 造 山 光 錦 都 京 本 日

9. Nippon ("Japan"). 日本

10. Satsuma

11. Satsuma

12. (Mon) Crest of House of Satsuma. On authentic pieces, this symbol appears in gosu blue.

13. (Mon) Crest of Kusonoki.

14. (Mon) Crest of Tokugawa.

Symbols found on Satsuma and Satsuma-style Wares

1. Two forms of waves.

2. Two forms of cloud formations.

3. A third form of cloud formation.

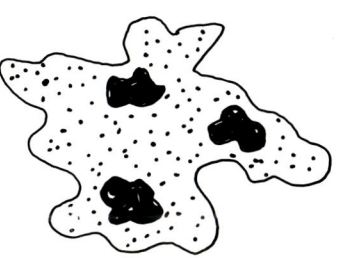

4. Kame (tortoise) symbols.

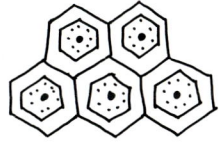

5. Flame symbols.   6. Coins.

Additional Symbols

Additional symbols, which are common to Satsuma and Satsuma-style wares. They are easy to recognize.

Mushroom	Represents long life
Peach	Symbol of marriage
Cherry blossoms	Symbolic of the Japanese people
Bamboo	Represents virtue
Benten	Only female goddess of the Seven gods of good luck. She represents charity.
Elephant	Symbolizes wisdom
Pine	Represents strength
Iris	The flower of victory
Chrysanthemum	Symbolic of purity
Peony	Symbolizes imperial power
Plum blossom	Symbolic of womanhood
Mt. Fujiyama	The celebrated Japanese mountain.

Helpful Hints

In evaluating age, color is a good aid. White or yellow outlines date from 1915. Decorative pieces having dark background colors and designs with gold outlines generally date from 1905. Gosu blue dates prior to 1870 and oxidized cobalt dates from 1870. The gold enamels used during the Edo period (1615-1868) were generally applied directly to the biscuit. There is a matte chocolate brown background on many of the Satsuma-style wares made during the 1920s. On similar wares produced during the 1930s, the matte brown backgrounds tend to be redder and lighter.

Satsuma-style wares have been mass produced since 1900. At the same time, production of Satsuma faience wares increased greatly. There are notable differences between Satsuma wares made during the Edo and Meiji periods and similar wares produced during the Taisho and Showa periods. On many of the later wares, the crackle is rather large and the lines of the crackle tend to be very long, irregular and greatly defined. On many of the later wares, the dark blue and dark green enamels are somber and the light colors tend to be too vivid and too intense.

Rim glazing is an aid for age evaluation too. Prior to 1900, the rims of covers were often left unglazed. During the Edo period, the entire undersides of lids and covers were generally left unglazed.

Color Photographs

All pairs have been photographed showing front and back views. The word Satsuma is used in descriptions to emphasize and explain specific types.

Photo # 1
Top row (left to right)

A pair of figural Satsuma vases. Taisho period, circa 1925. Height 6". This pair features haloed Arhats (disciples of Buddha) and Kwannon (deity). The haloes were given great emphasis. The border and side panels are oxidized cobalt blue, decorated with small gold flowers.

Bottom row

Figural Satsuma vase. Edo period, circa 1860. Height 25". Kara Shi Shi (lion-dog) handles with Tama (pearl or ball). The Shi Shi on the right is the female. Depicted are two Samurai warriors at the end of battle. Intricately detailed diapers form a delicate butterfly around the neck. Enamels include "silver".

Photo # 2
Top row
1. Koro (incense burner). Edo period, circa 1820. Height 9½". Kara Shi Shi finial. Center represents the Tama and is delicately decorated with phoenix and flowers, in pale enamels. The base is entwined with a dragon.

2. Tile. Edo period, circa 1830, 6" X 6". Delicately decorated with autumn flowers in pale enamels. Clouds were made of actual gold dust.

Bottom row
Pair of vases. Edo period, circa 1820. Height 8½". Most unusual contour with a double base. A five-petaled flower was cut out under the second base. Meticulously enameled in pale hues. Featured are irises, peonies, chrysanthemums, cherry blossoms and plum blossoms (Kinkozan).

Photo # 3
Top row —
1. Figural Satsuma plate. Edo period, circa 1850. Diameter 9½". Depicted on this plate are Arhats without haloes, enameled in pale hues. Nishikide diapers and dragons around the border. (Mon) Crest appears twice.

2. Figural Satsuma bowl. Edo period, circa 1850. Diameter 8". Featured are Buddha, Arhats and Kwannon. The inner border and exterior are gosu blue.

Bottom row —
1. Awaji Satsuma bottle. Edo period, circa 1830. Height 10½". Finely contoured and decorated in pale "transparent" enamels, with a straw yellow background. Neck and base have enameled phoenix birds; side panels feature dragons.

2. Awaji Satsuma bottle. Edo period, circa 1830. Height 10½". Phoenix birds and cloud formations decorate the neck and base. Featured is Tora (tiger). Enamels are pale and "transparent".

Photo # 4

Top Row —
Figural Satsuma charger. Edo period, circa 1850. Diameter 12½". This is the thousand-warrior design. (Mon) Crest appears twice on the border. Decorated with pale enamels. Nishikide diapers and dragons form the border designs.

Bottom row —
Ewers. Meiji period, circa 1895. Height 13". The lids have Kara Shi Shi finials and nishikide diapers. The swirling designs from the base to the neck represent the essence of aroma rising upwards. Well-contoured, with chain-like formations from the base to the spout.

Photo # 5

Top row —

1. Satsuma-style cup and saucer. Meiji period, circa 1900. The fluted cup has three legs. Decorated with Chinese scenes and nishikide diaper panels.

2. Satsuma-style demi-tasse. Showa period, circa 1935. A fine porcelain with brightly enameled flowers.

Second row —

1 & 3. Satsuma-style plates. Meiji period, circa 1910. Diameter 5″. Medallions of scenic designs and nishikide diapers.

2. Satsuma-style teapot. Meiji period, circa 1910. Height 5″. Medallions of scenic designs and nishikide diapers.

Third row —

Tea set. Meiji period, circa 1870. Height 4½″. Teapot, sugar and creamer have bamboo finials. Decorated with flying cranes. Fine brush work (Kinkozan)

Bottom row —

1. Box. Edo period, circa 1810. Diameter 5″. Decorated with floral sprays and butterflies. Gold enamel was sparingly applied, and used just to highlight the overall design. (Kinkozan)

2. Teapot. Edo period, circa 1800. Height 4½″. Kame finial, decorated with peonies in pale enamels. (Kinkozan)

3. Pitcher. Edo period, circa 1840. Height 4½″. Delicately enameled in pale hues. Featured are peaches and chrysanthemums. (Kinkozan)

Photo # 6
Top row —
1. & 2. Pair of figural Satsuma vases. Showa period, circa 1930. Height 5″. Haloed Arhats. (Mon) Crest appears on neck. Outlines have too few strokes, but basic design is well detailed.

3. Figural Satsuma bowl. Taisho period, circa 1925. Diameter 4½″. Haloed Arhats. (Mon) Crest appears on border four times. Same technique and styling as vases on this row.

Second row —
1. Awata Satsuma vase. Meiji period, circa 1910. Height 9″. Overall decorations of irises and butterflies. Five-petaled flower incorporated into handles. Finely shaded background.

2. Bottle. Meiji period, circa 1890. Height 7½″. Finely detailed faces of feudal lords. Overall decoration of nishikide diapers.

3. Pilgrim bottle. Meiji period, circa 1885. Height 8½″. Good contour, decorated with peonies. Neck, base and side panels are covered with cloud formations.

Bottom row —
1. Vase. Taisho period, circa 1910. Height 18″. Kirin handles. See plate # 16.

2. Vase. Edo period, circa 1810. Height 10″. Mushroom handles, autumn flowers and gold dusted clouds. Finely enameled with pale hues and gosu blue.

3. Mishima Satsuma urn. Meiji period, circa 1885. Height 16½″. Designs of chrysanthemums and butterflies. Nishikide diapers on neck and lid.

Photo # 7
Top row —
1. Vase. Taisho period, circa 1915. Height 8½". Neck is ornamented with knife cuts. Enamels daubbed on.

2. Figurine. Meiji period, circa 1900. Height 10½". Kwannon overall decorations of cloud formations.

3. Vase. Meiji period, circa 1895. Height 8½". Overall decorations of nishikide diapers, elephant head handles. Neck is ornamented with knife cuts.

4. Vase. Taisho period, circa 1925. Height 7". Well crafted. (molded design)

Second row —
1. & 2. Vases (pair). Meiji period, circa 1875. Height 7". Oxidized cobalt blue panels, cherry blossom scene.

3. Figural Satsuma bowl. Taisho period, circa 1925. Diameter 7½". Interior decorated with Arhats and Kwannon. The crackle is large and defined.

4. Vase. Taisho period, circa 1915. Height 7½". Decorated with mums and birds. Nicely shaded background.

Bottom row —
1. Vase. Taisho period, circa 1920. Height 9½". Enamels were daubbed on.

2. Vase. Taisho period, circa 1920. Height 12¾". Floral designs and birds. Unusual contour and well-shaded background.

3. Vase. Taisho period, circa 1915. Height 12½". Neck ornamented with knife cuts. Colors daubbed on.

4. Vase. Taisho period, circa 1925. Height 7½". Decorated with birds and wisteria in the old tradition.

Photo # 8
Top row —
1. Awata Satsuma vase. Meiji period, circa 1910. Height 10½". Unusual contour. Finely blended background shading, covered with flowers and diapers.

2. Awata Satsuma vase. Meiji period, circa 1900. Height 13". Heavily enameled irises, leaf-shaped handles; rim and base covered with nishikide diapers.

3. Vase. Meiji period, circa 1910. Height 12½". Decorated with chrysanthemums and gold enameled leaves. Nishikide diapers around neck.

Bottom row —
1. Vase. Taisho period, circa 1915. Height 14". Very effective background shading lends richness to the morning-glories. A five-petaled flower is incorporated into the handles.

2. Jar. Meiji period, circa 1885. Height 16". Kara Shi Shi handles and finial, three masked feet. Nishikide diapers incorporated into the garments of the Samurai general and officers. Nine-petaled chrysanthemum appears on the border of the upper base.

3. Mishima Satsuma vase. Meiji period, circa 1885. Height 13½". Floral decorations, small elephant head handles and shaded background carefully executed.

Photo # 9

Top row

1. Vase. Showa period, circa 1935. Height 10″. Unrealistically enameled flowers; colors are washed out.

2. Vase. Meiji period, circa 1890. Height 15″. Beautifully enameled azaleas are almost lifelike, with blue enamels representing irises. The background is delicately shaded and lends more realism to the flowers.

3. Vase. Showa period, circa 1935. Height 10½″. The design is poor, the flowers unrealistically enameled. The colors are smeared.

Bottom row —

Nishikide diaper Satsuma jardiniere. Meiji period, circa 1880. Height 12″, diameter 12″. This piece is intricately and meticulously decorated with repetitive patterns and geometric designs. Each of the three panels has a ringed rope handle. The interior panels are decorated with irises, peonies, and chrysanthemums.

Photo # 10
Top row —
1. Jar. Taisho period, circa 1920. Height 10". Kara Shi Shi handles and finial. Decorated with trailed enamels, and void of gold.

2. Figural Satsuma jar. Meiji period, circa 1875. Height 8½". Ringed Kirin handles. Extensive use of gold. Intricately detailed.

3. Figural Satsuma jar. Taisho period, circa 1915. Kara Shi Shi handles and final. Base and rim ornamented with cutouts.

Bottom row —
1. Vase. Taisho period, circa 1925. Height 15½". The poorly shaded background blends well with the unrealistically colored flowers. Compare plate #9, middle vase, top row.

2. Awata Satsuma jar. Meiji period, circa 1900. Height 17½". Kara Shi Shi-with-Tama finial, Kirin handles and three masked feet. Covered with medallions of intricately detailed peonies.

3. Figural Satsuma vase. Taisho period, circa 1920. Height 15½". Scenic design. Japanese beauties wearing kimonos which are greatly detailed. Snow-capped cherry blossoms.

Photo #11

Top row —

1. & 3. Figural Satsuma vases (pair). Meiji period, circa 1880. Height 3". Women and children entering a temple with the reverse covered with masses of peonies.

2. Mishima Satsuma vase. Meiji period, circa 1875. Height 3½". Intricately designed with quails and flowers.

Second row —

1. Koro (incense burner). Meiji period, circa 1875. Height 2½". Oxidized cobalt blue with panels of birds and peonies.

2. Covered jar. Edo period, circa 1820. Height 3¾". Decorated with nishikide flowers; (mon) crest in gosu blue appears under the base.

3. Vase. Meiji period, circa 1875. Height 3½". Unusual contour with delicately enameled barnyard scene.

Third row —

1. Teapot. Meiji period, circa 1885. Height 2½". It has a center band of finely enameled courtesans.

2. Figural Satsuma brush pot. Taisho period, circa 1925. Height 2". Heart-shaped panels of mother and children.

3. Teapot. Meiji period, circa 1875. Height 1½". Thousand-flower design. (mille fleur)

Bottom row —

1. Figural Satsuma vase. Meiji period, circa 1875. Height 5". Oxidized cobalt blue panels. Cherry blossom scene.

2. Vase. Meiji period, circa 1870. Height 5¼". Ducks nesting under cherry blossoms. Unusual black background with "silver" and gold flowers.

3. Figural Satsuma pitcher. Taisho period, circa 1920. Height 4½". Good contour, featuring panels of warriors.

PHOTO # 12
Top row —
1. Vase. Taisho period, circa 1920. Height 11½". Decorated with boldly outlined leaves. The rim is fluted and turned inward. The pale leaves have dark outlining, giving this piece depth.

2.&3. Figural Satsuma vases (pair). Taisho period, circa 1915. Height 12". unlike jar, plate #10, top, this pair was carefully enameled. There is extensive use of gold. Unusual employ of both white and yellow outlining.

Bottom row —
1. & 2. Figural Satsuma vases (pair). Taisho period, circa 1915. Exceptionaly well-enameled. One side decorated with flowers. It has fine brushwork. The figural side has gold enameling. For vases done in trailed enamels their background color is most unusual.

3. Vase. Meiji period, circa 1890. Height 12". Well-shaded background. Gold lines represent netting enclosures for the detailed, lifelike pansies.

Photo # 13
Top row —
1-4. Sauce plates. Edo period, circa 1800. Diameter 4". Beautifully decorated with iridescent, jeweled, enamels.

Second row —
1. Vases (pair). Showa period, circa 1935. Height 3½". Decorated with irises in the old tradition.

2. Figural Satsuma vase. Showa period, circa 1930. Height 3¼". It is decorated with bands of children, butterflies and phoenix birds.

3. Figural Satsuma vase. Meiji period, circa 1880. Height 3½". It features a grouping of feudal lords. Oxidized cobalt blue panels are decorated with gold flowers.

Third row —
1. Tea set. Taisho period, circa 1920. There are five handleless cups, a creamer and teapot. This set is intact and was made to conform to the old tradition of only five cups. It is delicately enameled.

Bottom row —
1. Satsuma-style base. Showa period, circa 1930. Diameter 5". Decorated with swirls of nishikide diapers.

2. Koro. Meiji period, circa 1900. Height 6". A matte black background. Kara Shi Shi handles and finial. Intricately enameled with gold wisteria.

3. Satsuma-style jar. Meiji period, circa 1900. Height 3¾". Fan-shaped panels of cranes. Calligraphy covers the interior surface of the jar.

Photo # 14

The vases pictured on this plate are quite accessible. They are all faience (pottery). This type of design is common to Satsuma-style wares as well. The pieces depicting haloed Arhats and Kwannon, which have scenic backgrounds, usually have yellow outlining.

Top row —
1. Vase. Taisho period, circa 1915. Height 12½". Good contour, nishikide diapers incorporated into garments.
2. Vase. Showa period, circa 1930. Height 8". Haloed Kwannon and Arhat.
3. Vase. Taisho period, circa 1920. Height 12½". Haloed Kwannon.

Bottom row —
1. Vase. Taisho period, circa 1925. Height 12½". Haloed Arhats and Kwannon with dragon. Green trailed enamels around base and near neck.
2. Vase. Taisho period, circa 1925. Height 15". Haloed Arhats only.
3. Vase. Taisho period, circa 1925. Height 12½". Depicts woman and child.

Photo # 15

Top row —

1. Awata Satsuma vase. Taisho period, circa 1915. Height 12″. Dark iron-red background decorated with irises and bold gold outlining.

2. Awata Satsuma vase. Meiji period, circa 1910. Height 12½″. Ringed Kara Shi Shi handles, dark green background, decorated with phoenix in bold gold enamel.

3. Awata Satsuma vase. Meiji period, circa 1905. Height 12″. Neck and rim are ornamented with cutouts.

Bottom row —

1. Awata Satsuma vase. Meiji period, circa 1900. Height 16½″. Kirin handles, fluted rim, extension on neck ornamented with cutouts.

2. Awata Satsuma vase. Meiji period, circa 1905. Height 15″. Neck and base decorated with nishikide diapers, detailed phoenix handles, heavily enameled irises with bold gold outlining.

3. Awata Satsuma vase. Meiji period, circa 1900. Height 16″. When turned sideways it has a definite outline of a fish (kissing gourami). Sea horse handles are the fins, a fish tail is the neck.

Photo # 16

Satsuma wares of this type are quite abundant. They were produced after 1900 in large quantities. They were exported to the United States as well as European countries. The figures that appear on this type of Satsuma vary but the style and technique used are always the same.

Top row —

1. & 2. Vases (pair). Meiji period, circa 1910. Height 12". Featuring geishas. Dotted enamels form fan and circular shapes.

3. Vase. Taisho period, circa 1915. Height 12". Well-contoured handles. Samurai general and officer.

Bottom row —

1. & 3. Vases (pair). Meiji period, circa 1905. Height 12". Ringed elephant handles, with two Samurai officers.

2. Vase. Meiji period, circa 1910. Height 18". The neck is ornamented with knife cutouts. Ringed tasseled handles.

Photo # 17
Top row —
1. Figural Satsuma vase. Meiji period, circa 1880. Height 2¼". Featuring scholar and students. Nishikide diapers around the neck and base.

2. Pair of scenic vases. Showa period, circa 1930. Height 1⅛. Showa period, circa 1930.

3. Satsuma-style salt. Showa period, circa 1930. Diameter 1¼". Interior and exterior are decorated with cherry blossoms and fans.

Second row —
1. Satsuma-style toothpick-holder. Showa period, circa 1930. Height 1¾". Intricately enameled with Rokkasen, the six poets.

2. & 3. Figural Satsuma box. Meiji period, circa 1875. Height 1¼". Interior of lid and base are enameled with cherry blossoms.
4. Satsuma-style toothpick-holder. Showa period, circa 1930. Height 2". Scenic panels, interiors decorated with landscape.

Third row —
1. & 3. Satsuma-style bowls. Showa period, circa 1930. Diameter 1¾". Decorated with jeweled enamels.

2. Figural Satsuma bowl. Taisho period, circa 1920. Diameter 4". Haloed Arhats, with one riding a flying phoenix.

Bottom row —
1. Figural Koro. Meiji period, circa 1880. Height 2¼". Heart-shaped panels of family groups.

2. Figural Koro. Meiji period, circa 1860. Height 2½". Panels of children, intricate blocks of nishikide diapers, with sixteen-petaled chrysanthemum near rim.

Photo # 18

All the wares on this plate are Satsuma-style. It is common to find that the gold enameled finials and handles on many Satsuma-style wares have a marbleized treatment. This method was employed to give an outward appearance of gold worn by age deterioration.

Top row —

1. Koro. Taisho period, circa 1925. Height 10". Three masked feet, Kara Shi Shi handles, Kara Shi Shi with Tama finial. Well-contoured cutouts on the cover.

2. Vase. Showa period, circa 1930. Height 7". Arhats and Kwannon, Kara Shi Shi handles.

Second row —

1. Teapot. Showa period, circa 1935. Height 7". Pagoda finial, molded sides.

2. Teapot. Showa period, circa 1930. Height 7". Mahoot (elephant driver) finial.

Bottom row —

1. Lamp base. Showa period, circa 1930. Height 7". Haloed Kwannon riding an elephant.

2. Teapot. Taisho period, circa 1925. Height 7". Pagoda finial, molded sides.

3. Lamp Base. Taisho period, circa 1925. Height 6". Elephant with pagoda finial.

Photo # 19

Each tea set pictured on this plate has twenty-one pieces. They are Satsuma-style.

Top row—

Showa period, circa 1935. Dragon finials and spouts. Decorated with Kwannon and Arhats. The porcelain is heavy and much of it is part of the overall design. Cups have luster interior.

Second row —

Taisho period, circa 1925. This set has dragon finials, spouts, handles and molded dragons around the serving pieces. Entire surface of the light, translucent porcelain is covered with designs. White trailed enamel was used to emphasize dragon and handles. Arhats and Kwannon with (mon) crest on each piece. Much dragon scale throughout.

Bottom row —

Showa period, circa 1930. Dragon finials and spouts, with the exception of the creamer. Porcelain is a fine quality and is completely covered with design. White trailed enamel used for emphasis, as above. Interior of cups have pearlized luster finish.

Photo # 20
Top row —
1. Figural Satsuma vase. Taisho period, circa 1920. Height 2½". Scholar and students, intricate and minute detailing.

2. Nishikide diaper Satsuma spill holder. Taisho period, circa 1920. Height 3¼". Minutely detailed. Three legs decorated with ladybugs.

3. Goblet. Taisho period, circa 1925. Height 2¾". Scene of mother and child is finely detailed.

4. Tea caddy. Meiji period, circa 1895. Height 3". Cover, inner lid and base have gold outlining.

Second row —
1. & 2. Satsuma-style salt & pepper. Taisho period, circa 1915. Height 3". Trailed enamels and scenic panels.

3. Koro. Meiji period, circa 1910. Height 2". Delicate scenes of mother and children.

4. & 5. Satsuma-style toothpick-holders. Showa period, circa 1930. Height 1¾". Intricately enameled with Sanju Rokkasen, the thirty-six poets.

Third row —
1. & 2. Vases. Meiji period, circa 1910. Height 3¼".

3. Bowl. Meiji period, circa 1895. Height 2½". (See plate 7, top row 1)

4. & 5. Salt and pepper. Showa period, circa 1935. Height 2¾".

Bottom row —
1. & 2. Figural Satsuma bowl. Edo period, circa 1865. 2" x 3". Gosu blue exterior. Beautifully detailed.

3. Vase. Meiji period, circa 1880. Height 3¾". Children in scenic panels. Peonies on reverse.

4. & 5. Vases (pair). Meiji period, circa 1900. Height 3". Cherry blossom scene with Mt. Fuji.

Photo # 21

All the pieces pictured on this plate are Satsuma-style.

Top row —
Gods of good luck. Showa period, circa 1935. Height 3½". Hotei, Daikoku, Bishamon, Fukurokuju, Jurojin, Ebisu.

Second row —
1. Vase. Showa period, circa 1950. Height 2½".
2. Koro. Showa period, circa 1930. Height 2½".
3. Koro. Showa period, circa 1935. Height 4½".
4. Koro. Taisho period, circa 1925. Height 4".
5. Koro. Showa period, circa 1935. Height 3½".

Third row —
1. Vase. Showa period, circa 1950. Height 2½".
2. & 3. Vases (pair). Showa period, circa 1930. Height 3".
4. & 5. Salt and pepper. Taisho period, circa 1925. Height 3".
6. Elephant figurine. Showa period, circa 1935. Height 3".

Bottom row —
1. Vase. Taisho period, circa 1925. Height 3".
2. Teapot. Showa period, circa 1935. Height 2½".
3. Vase. Showa period, circa 1935. Height 1¾".
4. Vase. Showa period, circa 1950. Height 2½".
5. Vase. Taisho period, circa 1925. Height 3".
6. Vase. Showa period, circa 1930. Height 2½".

Photo # 22
Top row —
  Satsuma-style tea set. Showa period, circa 1935. Twenty-one pieces in total. Dragon finials, spouts and molded dragons around the serving pieces. The blue background is swirled to represent waves.

Second row —
1. Satsuma-style saki bottle. Showa period, circa 1935. Height 6". A rather heavy porcelain, decorated with dragons and flames.

2. Satsuma-style demitasse service. Showa period, circa 1935. Fifteen pieces in total. A fine quality porcelain decorated with dragons and flames. It has an open creamer.

Third row —
  Satsuma-style juice set. Taisho period, circa 1925. Elephant juice pot with six matching tumblers. Interior of tumblers have a pearlized luster finish. Mahoot finial.

Bottom row —
1. Satsuma-style vase. Taisho period, circa 1925. Height 6½". Molded dragon's head with molded dragon around center.

2. Satsuma cookie jar. Taisho period, circa 1920. Height 9". Kara Shi Shi handles and finial. Haloed Arhats and Kwannon.

3. Satsuma-style planter. Showa period, circa 1935. Height 5".

Photo # 23
Top row —
1. Satsuma-style vase. Showa period, circa 1935. Exterior has a shaded blue luster finish, with a scenic design.

2. Satsuma-style loving cup. Showa period, circa 1935. Height 8½". Black base and brown backround, with haloed Arhat.

3. Satsuma-style vase. Showa period, circa 1935. Height 6". Orange luster finish on the band near base.

Second row —
1. Satsuma ashtray. Showa period, circa 1935. Diameter 3½".

2. Vase. Showa period, circa 1930. Height 3". Poorly decorated with trailed enamels.

3. Vase. Taisho period, circa 1915. Height 6". Good contour with poorly executed enameling and design.

4. Satsuma-style vase. Showa period, circa 1935. Height 2½". Delicately decorated with irises.

Bottom row —
1. Jar. Taisho period, circa 1920. Height 5½". Poorly decorated (see plate 7, row 1).

2. Vase. Taisho period, circa 1920. Height 6½". Poorly decorated with trailed enamels. (See plate #12, top row.)

3. Awata Satsuma jar. Taisho period, circa 1920. Height 5½". Good contour with poor detailing.

Photo # 24

Top row —

1. Plate. Showa period, circa 1930. Diameter 6½". Scenic design of two geishas. Plate set in woven straw basket.

2. Vase. Showa period, circa 1935. Height 4½".

3. Cup and saucer. Showa period, circa 1950. (Occupied Japan). Mon-crest appears on the saucer.

Second row —

1. Vase. Showa period, circa 1950 (Occupied Japan). Height 3½".

2. Vase. Showa period, circa 1950 (Occupied Japan). Height 4¼".

3. Vase. Taisho period, circa 1925. Height 3½". Good enameling and design. (Mon) Crest appears on the saucer.

Third row —

1. Vase. Showa period, circa 1930. Height 5". Small black bands around base and neck. Good contour and design.

2. Bowl. Taisho period, circa 1925. Diameter 5". Lovely scenic design. Bowl set in woven straw basket.

3. Vase. Showa period, circa 1935. Height 5".

Bottom row —

1. Candy dish. Showa period, circa 1935. Diameter 7". Orange background is offset by the flowers and leaves.

2. & 3. Coasters. Taisho period, circa 1920. Diameter 3½". Haloed Arhats and Kwannon, carefully decorated. (Mon) Crest appears on each piece.

GLOSSARY

Arhats
Elderly men, disciples of Buddha. They have elongated ear lobes, and are usually shown with haloes around their heads.

Awaji Satsuma
A faience, finely crackled, with a yellow-cream color, often decorated with transparent enamels.

Awata Satsuma
A faience, finely crackled, with a gray-cream color and usually decorated with a profuse amount of gold enamel.

Bishamon
One of the seven gods of good luck. He represents glory.

Diaper
A repetitive pattern.

Dragon
One of the four supernatural animals. The Japanese dragon has three claws and is usually surrounded by flame or lightning symbols.

Dragon Scale
White enameled dots found on many types of Satsuma. Also, the name of Satsuma wares glazed with dark colors and covered with white dots.

Ebisu
One of the seven gods of good luck. He represents abundance of food.

Figural Satsuma
Satsuma wares decorated with warriors, saints or human figures.

Fukurokuju
One of the seven gods of good luck. He represents longevity.

Gosu Blue
The native blue-black and blue-gray.

Hotei
One of the seven gods of good luck. He represents contentment.

Jurojin
One of the seven gods of good luck. He is similar to Fukurokuju and represents long life.

Kame
The tortoise, one of the four supernatural animals. Its symbol is often found in diapers and it represents longevity.

Kara Shi Shi
The lion-dog. If shown in pairs, the one with the open mouth is the female.
Kirin
One of the four supernatural animals. It has one horn.
Kwannon
The Bodhisattva (deity) of Mercy.
Mahoot
An elephant driver.
Mishima Satsuma
Satsuma wares into which the designs were incised or impressed and then filled with enamel.
Mon
A symbol representing a family name. (Crest)
Nishikide
Masses of colors covering almost the entire surface.
Nishikide Diaper Satsuma
Masses of repetitive patterns covering almost the entire surface.
Oxidized Cobalt Blue
A blue-violet, used after 1870.
Phoenix
One of the four supernatural animals.
Rokkasen
The six poets, one woman and five men.
Sanju Rokkasen
The thirty six poets.
Satsuma
A finely crackled, cream-colored faience, decorated with raised enamels.
Satsuma-style
Porcelain wares with raised enameled decorations.
Tama
The ball (pearl or jewel) associated with the Kara Shi Shi.
Tora
The tiger.

Bibliography

The Pageant of Japanese History by Marion Day Dilts, 1938

Japanese and Oriental Pottery by Hazel H. Gorham, 1952

Handbook of the Pottery and Porcelain of the Far East by R. L. Hobson, 1937

Porcelain by Edward Dillon, 1904

Legend In Japanese Art by Henri L. Joly, 1967

Pottery and Porcelain by Warren Cox, 1944

Japanese Ceramics of the Last 100 Years by Irene Stitt, 1974

The Ceramic Art by Jennie S. Young 1878